let possibility rain dance above the grass

as if by magic

poems 2015-2019

Leah Elliott Hamilton

Copyright © 2020 by Leah Elliott Hamilton

The author gives permission for this work to be reproduced and distributed, in whole or in part, for any not-for-profit purpose, as long as her authorship is properly acknowledged.

Editing, design, and photos by Leah Elliott Hamilton, except for author photo

Author photo by Kristopher Hamilton

Cover photo and design by Leah Elliott Hamilton

www.leahielliott.com

ISBN 978-0-578-69851-9

The revolution is not yet, but is imminent.

For Kristopher

CONTENTS

Manifesto	1
between	2
born again	3
the blue wheelbarrow	5
And it occurred to her	6
It seems to me	8
Like a tree	9
So you know	11
Meet me at the park	12
the perilous art of rebirth	13
this perilous walk	14
love rise	15
For a limited time only!	16
whole	19
If we wish to have any hope at all	20

why judge	21
Affirmations to clear the scales from our eyes and usher in new light for our world	23
Birdlove	25
Birdsong	26
The light after a storm	27
Aftermath	29
Like romance	31
bloom	32
Whenever I find feathers	34
how alive we are	36
the family of stars	37
Open Borders	39
The meat of friendship	43
The unavoidable terror	44
your heart's whole song	49

as if by magic	50

~ ~ ~ ~ ~ ~ ~ ~ ~

poems for Kristopher

floor dance	53
Dispersit	54
I'll walk you home, you walk me home	57
Hope Springs	62
above the ache of the world	64
Acknowledgements	67

Manifesto

May the oppressed go free
to release the Creation
lying fallow and frozen within.

between

There is a line
between
connection and intrusion
and it is a barbed wire fence
That says to most organisms
"Keep out" and "Don't press there"

But to seeds carried on the wind:
"Come over as you will
and let the sister of what is growing in that heart
begin
to take root in mine"

And to the right kind of animal,
agile and careful,
"Slip through."

born again

I am born to be a poet.

And a poet tells the Truth:
The truths we know but have forgotten
The truths we know but do not want to know
The truths we know and didn't know we knew,
but whose revelation makes us
weep
with recognition
the same way we will weep
when reunited
with the Mother
from whom we were stolen

at birth.

the blue wheelbarrow
        after William Carlos Williams

so much depends
upon

a blue wheel
barrow

poised for
rubble from
beneath what was the kitchen.

And if occurred to her

And it occurred to her as the cold, hard wood of the pew dug into her shoulder blades and pinched off circulation at the backs of her thighs that the Church was not unlike a zombie: all of its parts moving more or less as they should

except for the breath

which didn't move at all, and the eyes, senseless and stagnant in their sockets. And as the ruddy priest expostulated on about sin and grace—but more about sin—she thought: *There must be a way of extracting the necessary meaning for my life that's more attuned, more innate, more efficacious than fracking through this wasteland.*

And her thighs unstuck and rose off the bench, and her feet pivoted toward the aisle, and her legs and torso followed her feet over the stone floor toward the dusty beams of sunlight at the back door. And she pried the door open onto a world of blue skies and gnats and passing traffic and green grass littered with pale pink blossoms. And the breath of the Earth lifted and swayed through her and filled her lungs and veins from her throat to her toes.

And she swayed with the Breath, and began to dance...

it seems to me

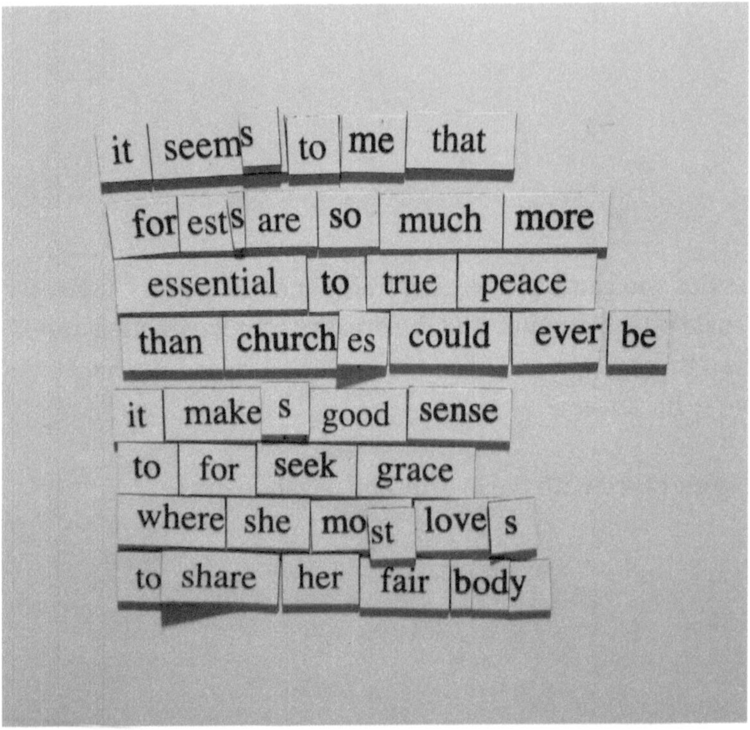

it seems to me that
forests are so much more
essential to true peace
than churches could ever be
it makes good sense
to for seek grace
where she most loves
to share her fair body

Like a tree

I asked God:

"How do I wear beauty with neither arrogance nor apology?"

She answered:

"Like a tree."

so you know

meet me at the park

Dedicated to the community of the Really, Really Free Market of Carrboro, North Carolina.

the perilous art of rebirth

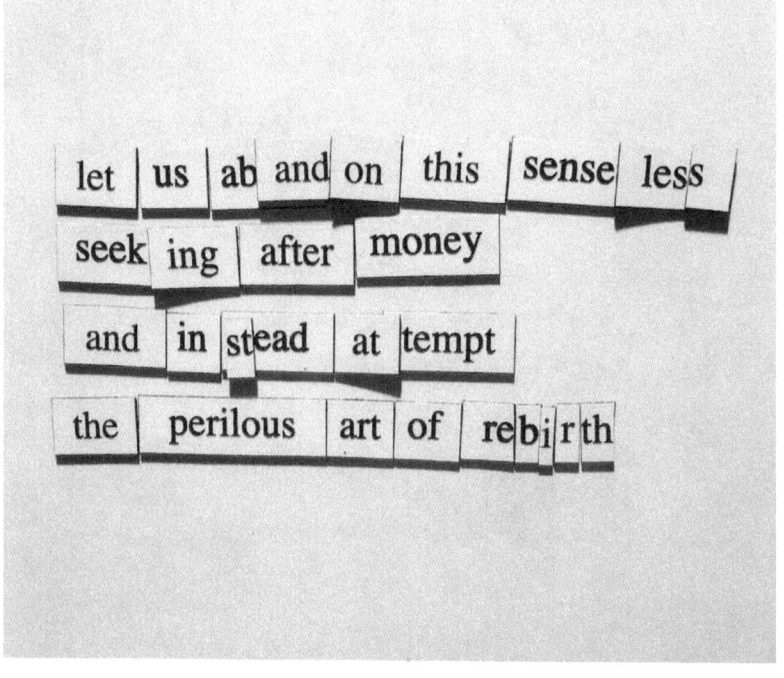

this perilous walk

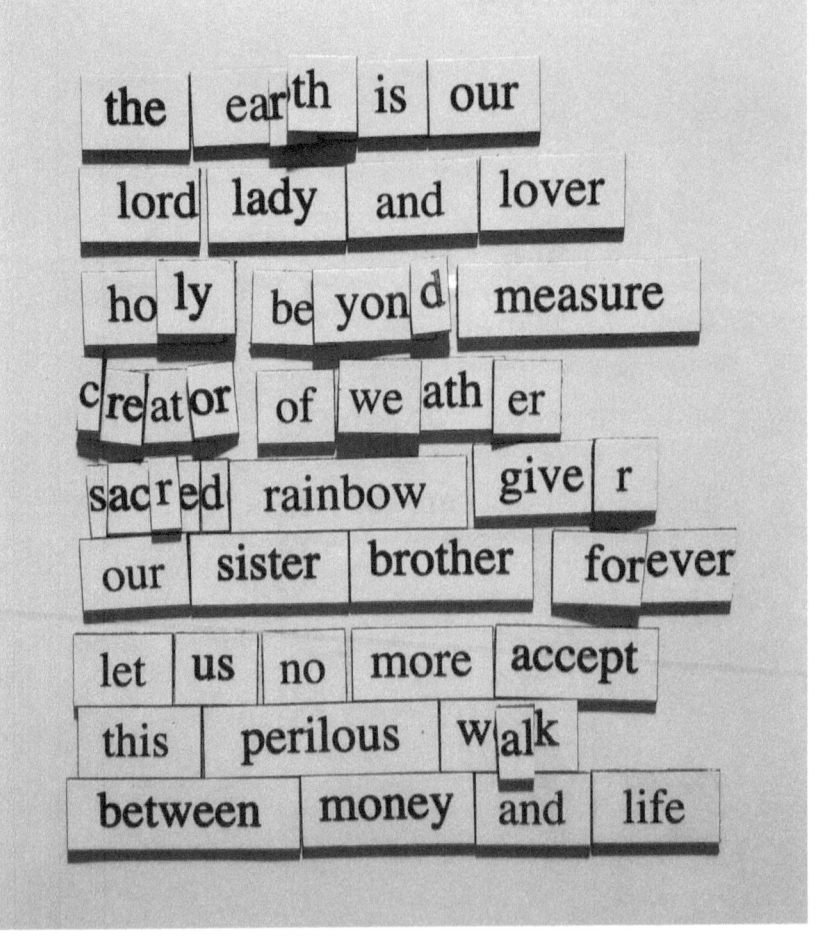

the earth is our
lord lady and lover
holy beyond measure
creator of weather
sacred rainbow giver
our sister brother forever
let us no more accept
this perilous walk
between money and life

love rise

I wander barefoot
up on the body
of my mother
with nothing between
her grass and me
I feel her love rise
through me from beneath
filling heart soul & lungs
with our daily breath
of light laughter
and life

For a Limited Time Only!

O say does that war-tangled Bannon yet prey
o'er the Land of the Free Gift with Purchase!
and the home of the KKK?

Where Congress shall make no law respecting
an establishment of religion,
with the exception of the Almighty LORD Dollar

In this God we trust

that all men are created equal
And therefore, the only way to keep more than your share
is to cheat
with loopholes that aren't just good. They're grrrrrrrreat!
How do you spell tax relief for the rich?

My oppressor has a first name
It's G-R-E-E-D.

My oppressor has a second name
It's gross inequity.

Exploititol® is not for everyone.

Side effects may include receding shorelines, permanent species loss, toxic rivers, loss of mountaintops, fallen forests, increased global temperature, military bloating, wage slavery, bank bailouts, corporate welfare, police brutality, mass shootings, mass incarceration, opioid addiction, life-threatening legislation, and more frequent rumination.

Talk to your doctor
if you experience
liberal heart-bleeding
or thoughts of regicide,
as these may be signs of a more serious sedition.

But wait! There's more!

Nuclear operators are standing by,
and 15 minutes couldn't save you,
or anyone that you love.

Can you hear me now?

Good.

Because our chance to SAVE BIG!

ends soon.

For a limited time only
can acquiescence be shattered.

For a limited time only
we may yet avert the worst.

For a limited time only
we have breath in our bodies.

Act. Now.

whole

How we long to be whole
all these disparate parts
that should not be so.

If we wish to have any hope at all

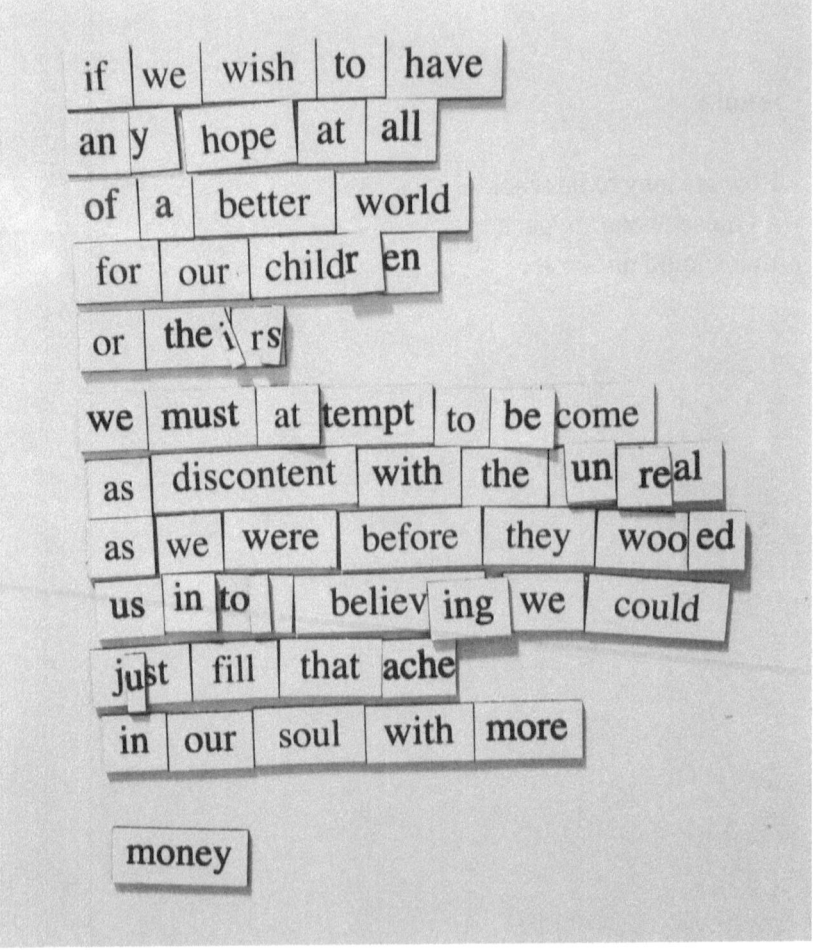

if we wish to have
any hope at all
of a better world
for our children
or theirs
we must attempt to become
as discontent with the unreal
as we were before they wooed
us into believing we could
just fill that ache
in our soul with more

money

why judge

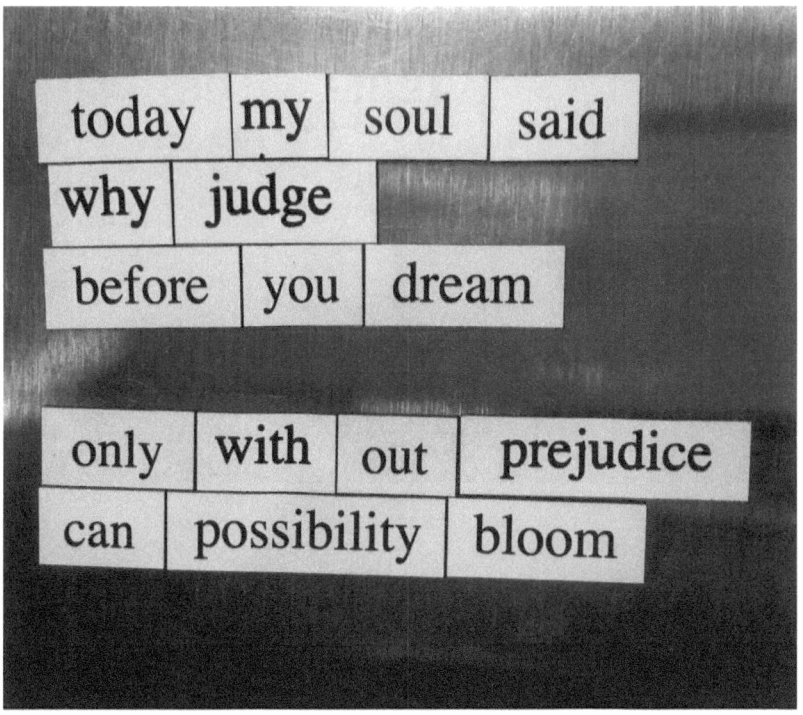

I
believe
d e light from
the friend
kiss es the world
alive

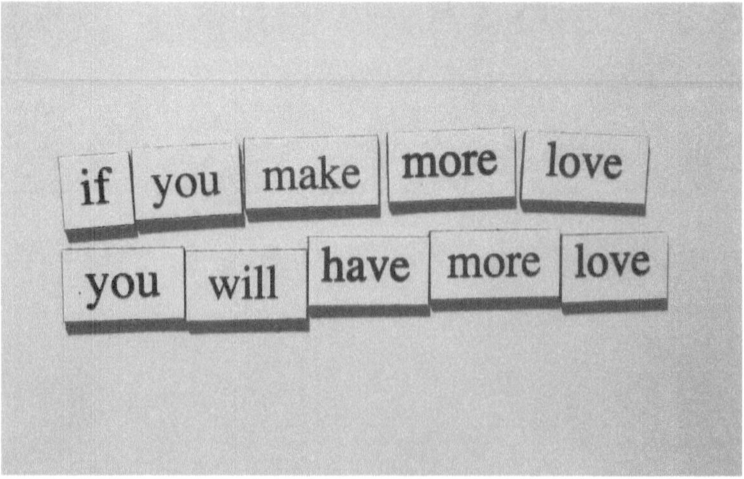

if you make more love
you will have more love

Affirmations to clear the scales from our eyes and usher in new light for our world

I will nurture narratives that affirm my vitality and my worth.

I will let myself be seen.

I will use my voice to awaken awareness of truth.

I will open my heart as a conduit for the currents of love all around asking to be let flow where they need to go to heal this world of its hurts and harms till we lay down arms at last and cast aside this pride that makes us hide our fear of the end of this ride. The river is wide, and we're all in it and of it and are it, forever.

So hold my hand. Let's stick together.

Birdlove

Faith in the birds
It asks so little
of me
Yet fills me with as
much
Comfort and Joy as
Jesus
used to.

And sometimes still does.

bird song

The light after a storm

A poet must go outside
for at least ten minutes a day,
no matter the weather.

It is a mercy of the kind that leads
me to continue
to believe
in a force of Love in the universe
that there is no light more beautiful
than the light after a storm.

Pristine, piercing, fragile it falls
out of postpartum clouds
still heavy with their rumbling
remnants of rain,
aching for release.

That this light filtered through
gray travail
is of such unsurpassed beauty
strikes me as an intentional
effort at maintaining cosmic
equilibrium.

On days when I'm paying attention,
anyway.

You must breathe unconditioned
air
if you want to think unconditioned
thoughts,
speak unconditioned
words,
feel unconditioned
Love,
stand midwife to the unconditioned
Light
breaking into the world.

Aftermath

Resist the urge to analyze.
It does no good.
Instead, try opening.
Try surrendering,
although the very nature of
trying
inevitably impedes surrender.

Try asking.

Love of all that is, seen and unseen:
Teach me to be a willing recipient
of bounty and beauty.
Let generosity condense around
my heart
like dew in the dark night.
Let it drip and cleanse
and heal and nourish.

Let grace be as my day,
a warm radiance ripe
for the basking

unearned
and undeserved as the sun

and just as freely offered.

Bellow forth blossoms among
the fecund fumes rising from
scorched earth
till sweet smells alchemize
the breath in my throat
from its gripping sadness
into flowering song.

All is well. All is well.

like romance

like romance
possibility will hide
then breathe light
so strong and kind

trust the good
of our common soul
like shining bird song
accept every surprise
or lack there of

bloom

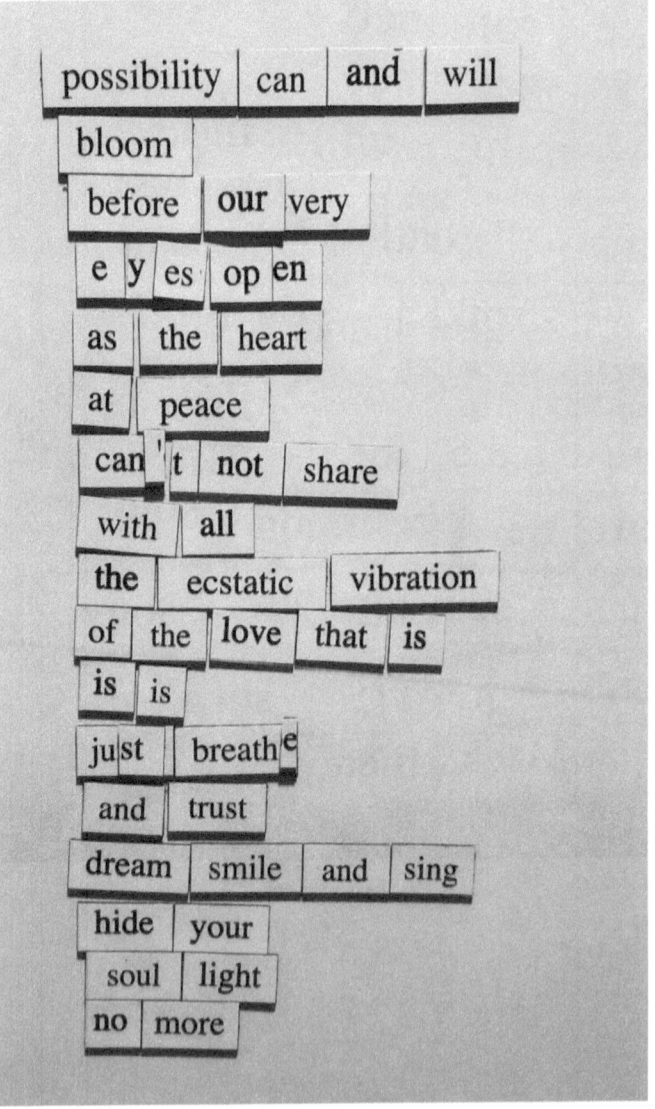

possibility can and will
bloom
before our very
eyes open
as the heart
at peace
can't not share
with all
the ecstatic vibration
of the love that is
is is
just breathe
and trust
dream smile and sing
hide your
soul light
no more

Whenever I find feathers

Whenever I find feathers,
it makes me feel smiled upon.
It makes me smile.

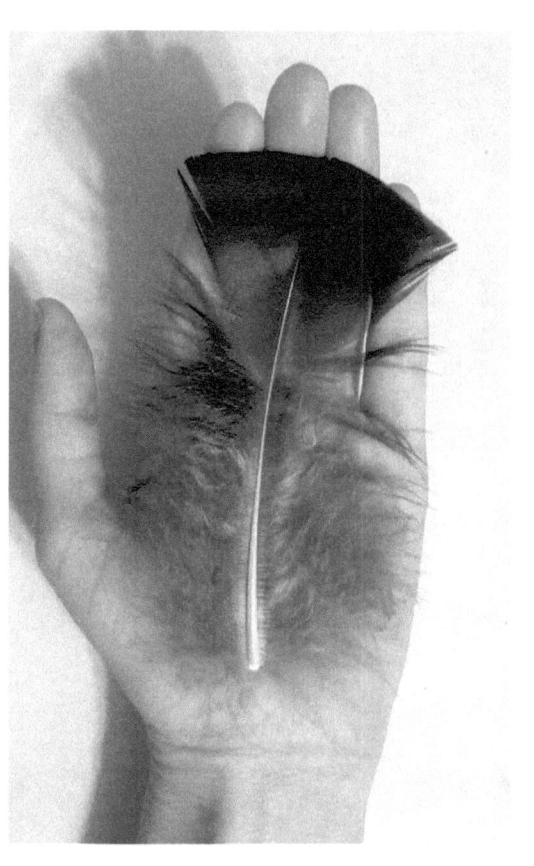

how alive we are

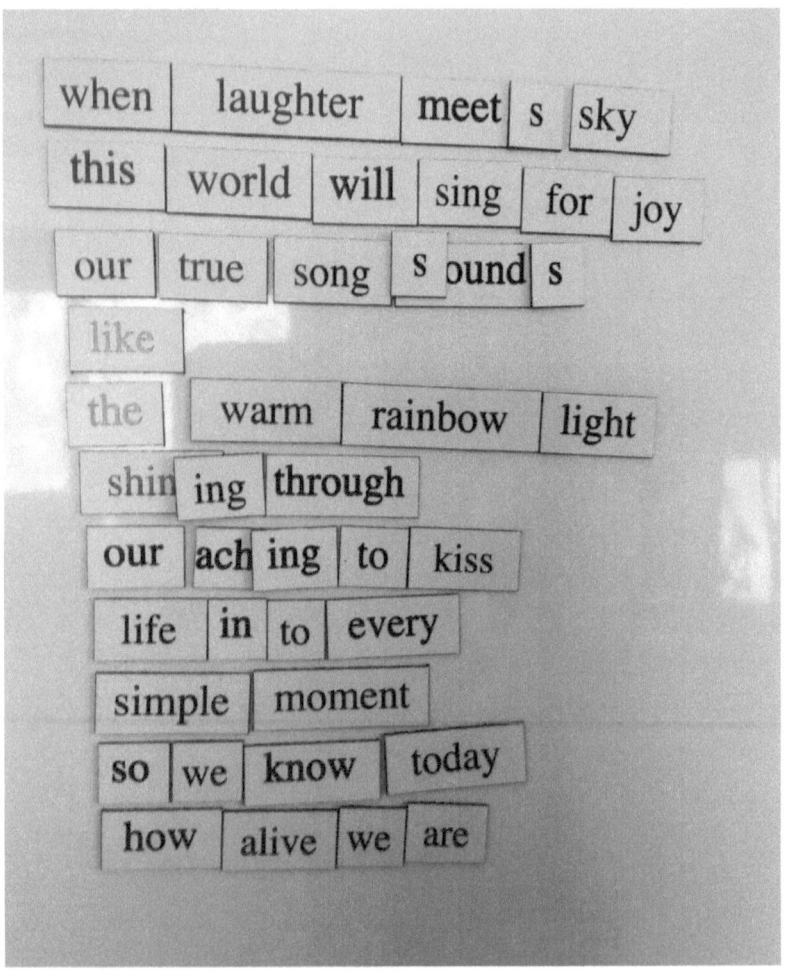

when laughter meets sky
this world will sing for joy
our true song sounds
like
the warm rainbow light
shining through
our aching to kiss
life into every
simple moment
so we know today
how alive we are

the family of stars

you should know
you are a member
of the family of stars
from before time was

you are the light and material
of the oldest and newest
creations

your heart is where
the dream and dance of every sky
beneath death
exist for real at last

sunshine
lives within us all
to yield its light and warmth
all we need do is open
to our heart's wisdom
and always dare
to follow

Open Borders

I once had a student who moved like water,
so much so that one morning, when she came in out of the rain,
I could barely tell where the drops of rain ended and she began.
And when she spoke, I could barely tell where she ended and her words began.
"I remember something on the bus," she said. "Tell me if I translate it right.
Long ago, I hear teaching that say: Life is short.
We all of us die. We know that is true. So because this is true, we also know
that all we have time to do is love.
Is that right?"
This truth she dropped into my lap had the weight and the urgency
of a newborn infant.
"Yes," I told her. "That is exactly right."
And I will tell you now another truth:
If you look at our Earth as it really is, without the invented map lines,
you cannot tell where one nation ends and another begins.
And if we look at each other as we really are,
you cannot tell where one heart ends and another begins,

so much so that if you are not okay, then neither am I.
And so I need you to do this:
Stop inventing borders between human hearts.
We don't have time for that.
Instead, I need you to, as best as you can,
do all you can to love
every rising and falling wave of humanity
you have the opportunity to swim through.
This can be hard with people with whom we disagree,
but if you are like me—and experience has taught me that you are—
it is often even harder with the people with whom you are closest.
I need you to keep trying anyway,
and I promise that I will too.
Open your arms. Open your hearts. Open the borders.

For all of my ESL students

Happy Valentine's Day
Happiness Always

To Ms Leah:

May your every day be filled with flowers and luckiness.

❇ Ling Ling

remember

death is real

all we have time to do is love

the meat of friendship

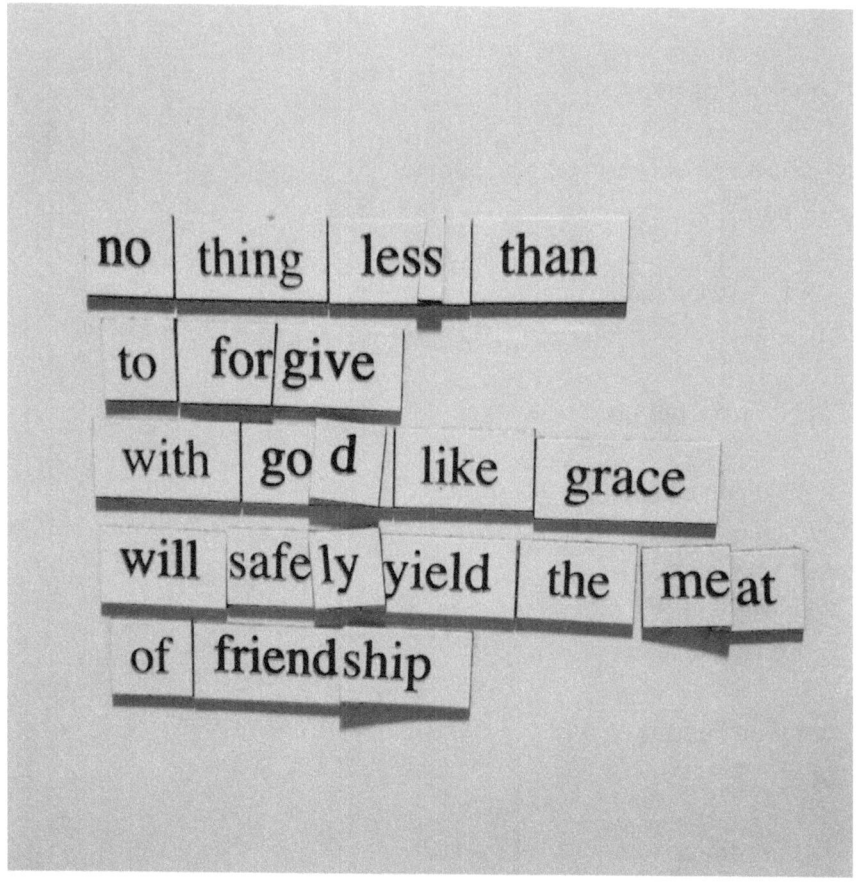

The unavoidable terror

I have oh so many words to express
grief and suffering.

I can oh so poetically tell you about
my pain.

I am oh so good at articulating
sorrow.

Here. Check out my latest iteration:

It's like I'm clinging to a sheer
cliff face,
trying to climb.
And sometimes I do manage to raise
myself a few meters
up
but then I oh so reliably and predictably
fall,

farther down from where I started
(of course),
knock my chin,

scrape up my chest and limbs,
bloody my fingers.
And I can't see the top.
I can't even see the bottom.
I've been at this for so long,
I'm beginning to think that the cliff face
is all that there is.

Vivid, isn't it?
Gets you right in the feels, doesn't it?

I am oh so good at articulating
sorrow,
and I am oh so tired of doing so.

So much so,
I may finally be willing
to let go
of this cliff face,
push back
into freefall.

Maybe I'll even learn to embrace
the unavoidable terror

for long enough to reach
terminal velocity,
zero gravity,
and just float for awhile
before I slam into
the bottom
that is coming for us all.

I'm beginning to consider
letting go,
pushing back
from this cliff face.
I'm beginning to believe
that even falling
might be better than this
clinging.

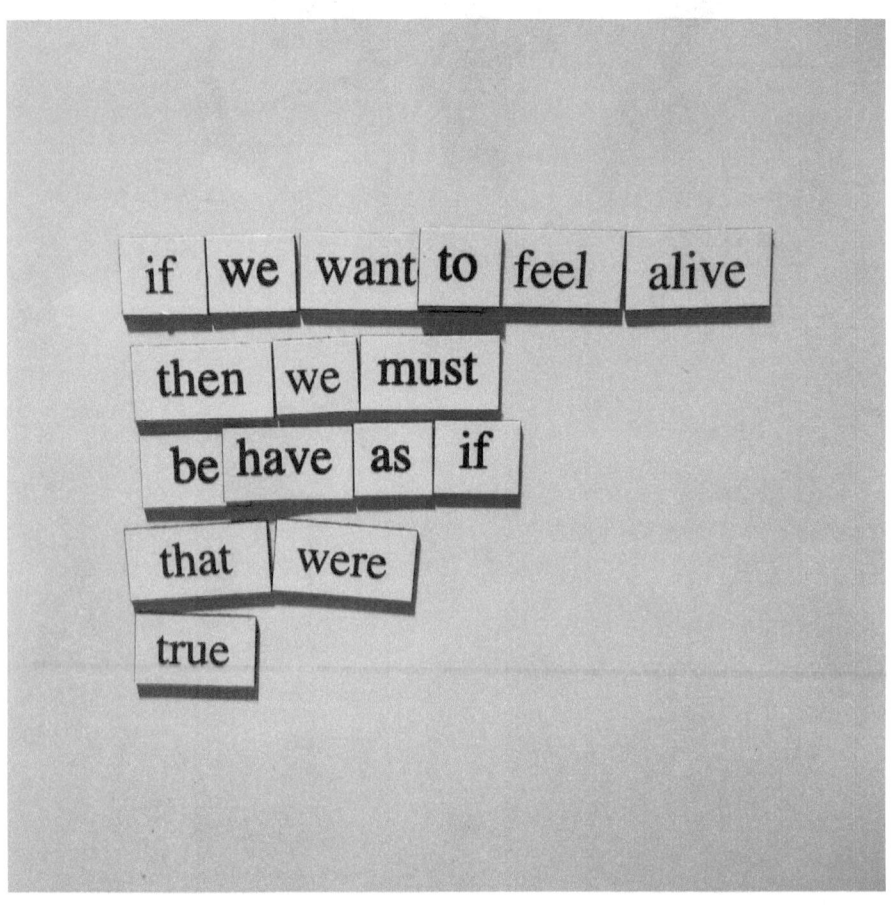

your heart's whole song

you can begin to at one for
the lies you have believed

by dancing to the beat of your
heart's whole song
that's how our seeds of possibility
will meet the blue sky
at last

as if by magic

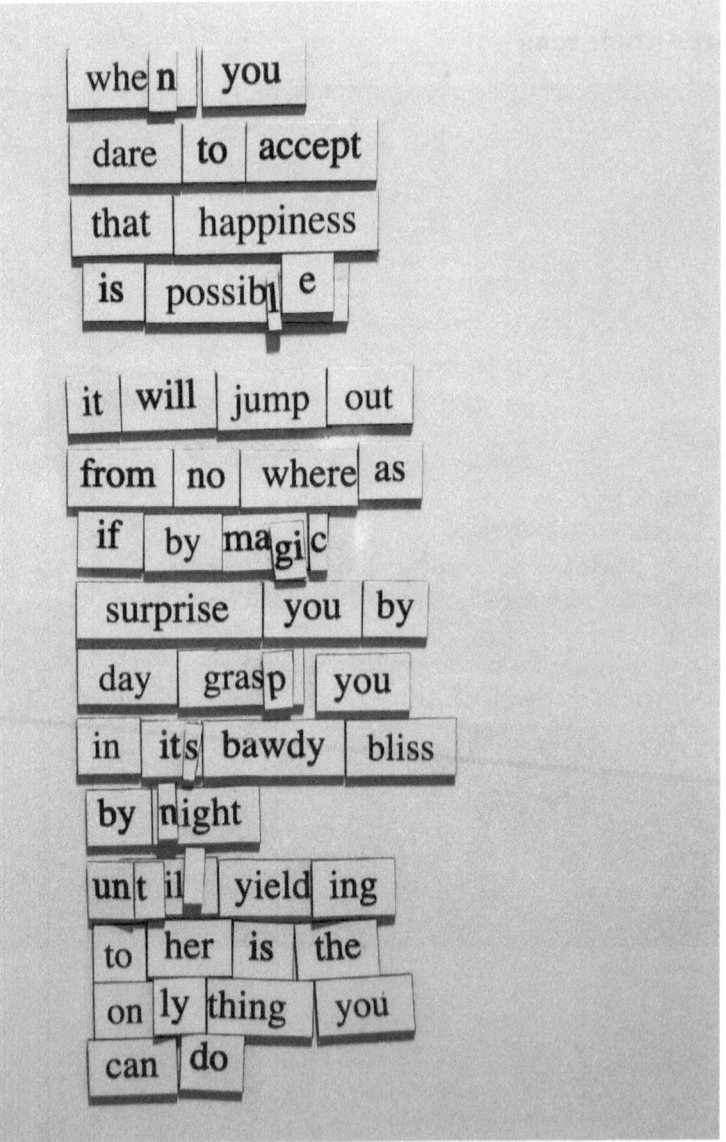

when you
dare to accept
that happiness
is possible

it will jump out
from no where as
if by magic
surprise you by
day grasp you
in its bawdy bliss
by night
until yielding
to her is the
only thing you
can do

poems for Kristopher

floor dance

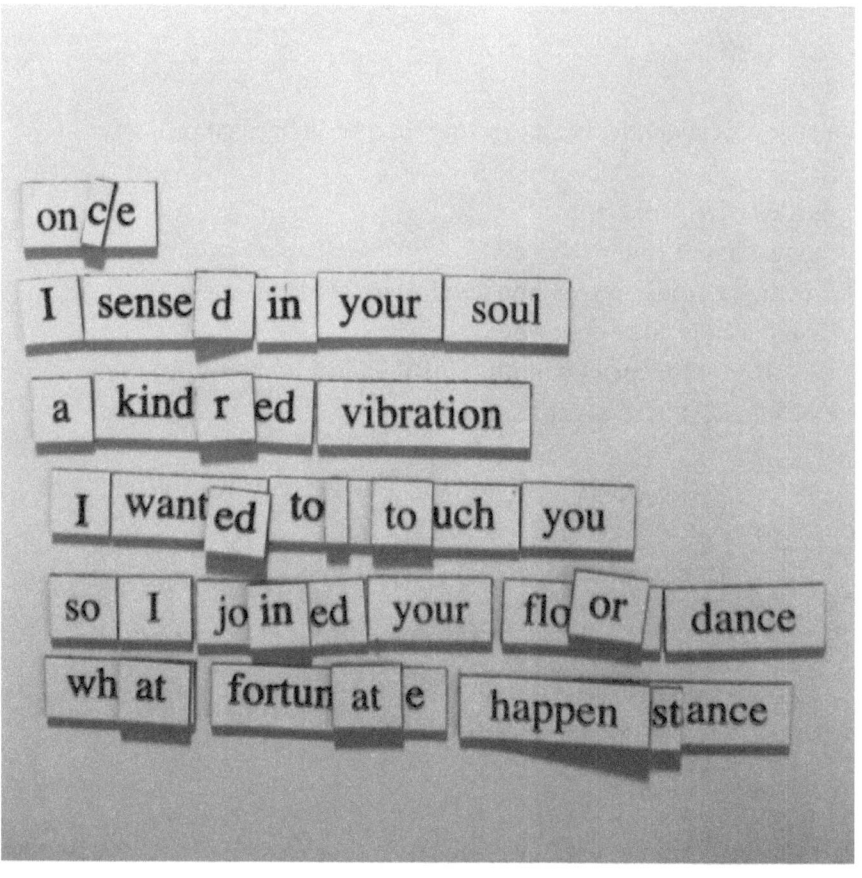

Dispersit

You and I have now been together long enough to go through three
bottles of tequila
longer than it sounds since
I mean the ones I buy in one point seven five liter casks.
Cheaper per ounce that way
thriftiness my Mormon mother instilled in a home whose filmy residue still sticks to my skin.

     *   *   *

I know a Honduran woman whose face radiates kindness
the same way that milk
and honey does. I teach her English with pop songs. She asks if the 'ache' in 'heartache'
is the same as the 'ache' in 'headache'
I say yes and wince
at the lie. I remember the excruciating
shine over her eyes
when she told me that she has not

been to her own country
for fourteen years
          *and my mother die three years ago and I
never see her again*

Where can home possibly be?

I have been unmoored for quite some time now
and you, too, my love
are in
exile.

              *   *   *

I watch you in your half-lit living room, dancing around and playing
the bass and I think you're so sexy but not
the thin, watery, popstar kind of sexy.
You're the kind of sexy with all the texture and the weight
and the reality of a thick
stew.

I didn't know that you loved Tori Amos so much and your
rapture makes me wish
that I had stuck with the piano. I bask happy in your

        scattering
of sound and vitality
        until

the thought surfaces
like a cockroach
swimming up through sifted flour:

I remember
that one day you will die

and I realize
that I now care about this.

I see it: a slit of the yellow light of Home
falling out of a gray stone wall

and I go in.

I'll walk you home, you walk me home

Because even before we spoke,
once you entered my subconscious,
you never really left.

Because you've read so many books,
maybe even more than I have.

Because you once told me that I remind you of
Jane Goodall,
and no one has ever praised me so highly in all
my life.

Because we each define where we're from
in terms of the land,
not the municipalities.

Because you are expansive enough to receive me
in all my intensity.
Because your intensity stretches my own
capacity for spaciousness.

Because I have decided to let you be the person who sees me in full.
Because I want to do my best to see you in full.

.

Because from the moment I first reached for you, our whole bodies fit so well together.
The clay in me knows the clay in you.

Because you introduced me to Saul Williams
and because you're okay with it that I'd like to sleep with him,
because you'd kind of like to sleep with him too.

Because we live in a world gone mad,
and you are the sanest person I know.

Because you are the kind of person who will get out of your car and cry over the deer with whom you could not avoid colliding, and hold him in your arms until he dies.

Because your cock feels like the reason I was put on this earth.

Because you know all the plants.
Because you know them like friends.

Because you find God in the same places I do.
Because one of those places is between our thighs.
Because another is Hafiz.
Because another is any clear, cold
mountain stream.

Because you show me the way home to myself,
as many times as necessary.

hope springs

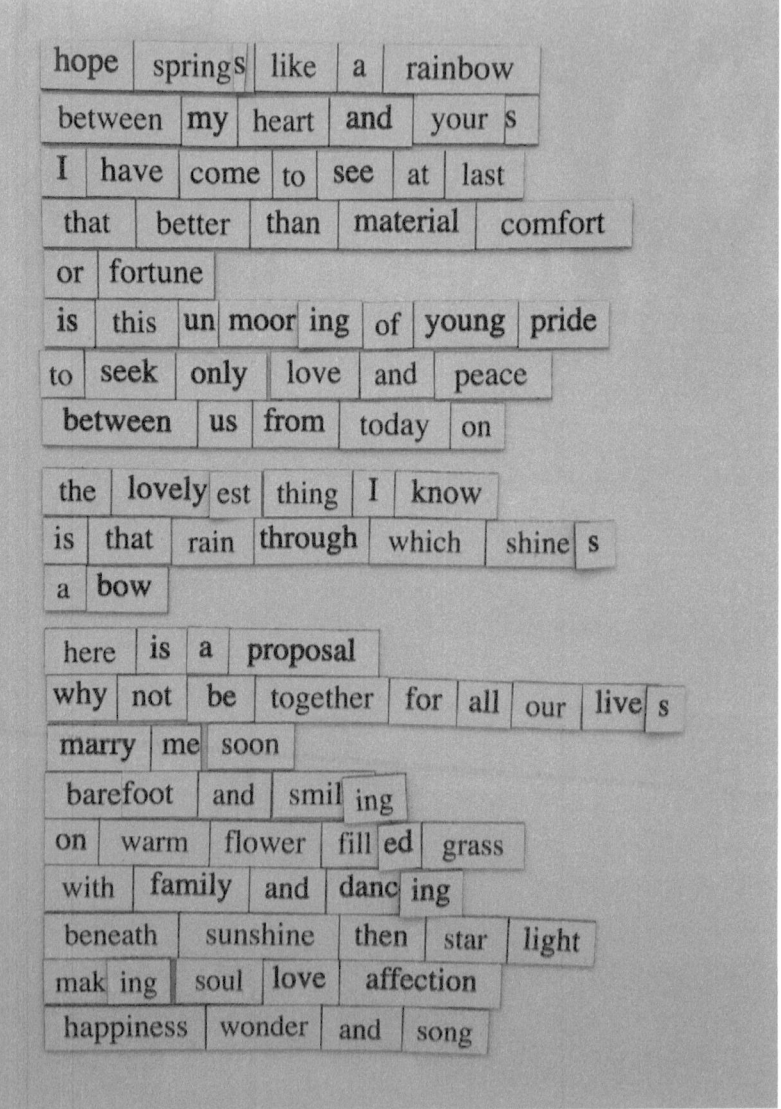

hope springs like a rainbow
between my heart and your s
I have come to see at last
that better than material comfort
or fortune
is this un moor ing of young pride
to seek only love and peace
between us from today on

the lovely est thing I know
is that rain through which shine s
a bow

here is a proposal
why not be together for all our live s
marry me soon
barefoot and smil ing
on warm flower fill ed grass
with family and danc ing
beneath sunshine then star light
mak ing soul love affection
happiness wonder and song

my heart friend let's dream
a new hope of happiness
in to old age
we could call it the possibility
of the laughter we could meet
each day when we kiss
or taste the breath of our world

say you will share your life
with me and I will sing for joy
at being alive to feel this warmth
so ecstatic so simple & true
as I follow only my essential vibration
which always arrives at you

above the ache of the world

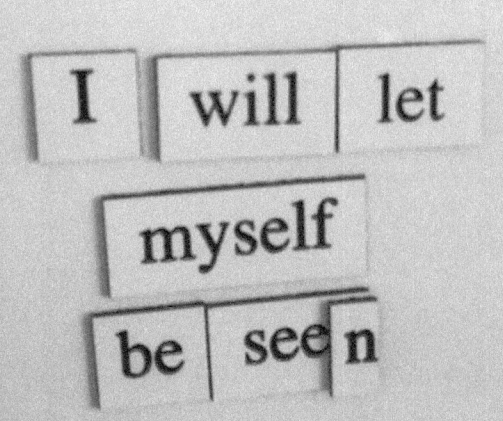

Acknowledgements

No one accomplishes anything of value all on their own, and I offer my gratitude to all who played a part in bringing this volume into existence.

To Mary Oliver, Joy Harjo, and Saul Williams for forming my personal holy trinity of three favorite poets, for living lives of truth, and for putting your work out into the world, where it could sustain, edify, and inspire me.

To the community of the Really, Really Free Market of Carrboro, North Carolina, for providing a space where I could practice my art, make connections, and refine my purpose.

To the Carrboro Poets Council for organizing the West End Poetry Festival every year, an event from which I have drawn much strength, solace, connection, and motivation.

To readers on social media who took the time to tell me that something I wrote meant something to them.

And for Kristopher Hamilton, my husband, my best friend and lover, my partner in Life, Love, and Creation. There is as much of you in these pages as there is of me, and I could not have created this book without you. Thank you for your relentless insistence on living in truth. Poetry is the art of truth-telling, and one cannot be a truth-teller without also being a truth-liver. You are well aware that I am not always happy about your commitment to truth. At times it is uncomfortable, even excruciatingly so, but the sane part of me always knows that a commitment to absolute truth is ultimately a gift. Thank you. I love you.

ABOUT THE AUTHOR

Leah Elliott Hamilton is an embodied speck of the Tao, currently moving in the roles of partner, lover, mother, stepmother, teacher, writer, and poet. To find out more, look inside your own soul for the Universal Light within us all.

www.ingramcontent.com/pod-product-compliance
Lightning Source LLC
Chambersburg PA
CBHW021959290426
44108CB00012B/1135